MONTESSORI IN A NUTSHELL

D1323656

1

Dr. Maria Montessori

"Her [Maria Montessori] ideas were formulated after she had laboriously observed the needs of the individual child. Her goal was to develop the whole personality of the child, and her system is based on her strong belief in the spontaneous working of the human intellect. Her three primary principles are observation, individual liberty, and preparation of the environment." 1986
Hainstock, E. The Essential Montessori

4

Dr. Maria Montessori was born in Ancona, Italy in 1870. At the age of two she moved to Rome. She grew up under the influence of a traditional father and an ambitious strong-minded mother. She wanted to be an engineer but found being a woman was an obstacle. However she entered university and qualified as the first woman medical doctor in Italy. Her years of study taught her to survive under difficult circumstances. The ethics of the time did not allow for male and female students to work on human bodies at the same time so Maria had to return to the morgue *alone* at night to do her research. When she qualified she worked for some time caring for the poor in Rome. She was always interested in children, their health and the living conditions which affected health. Around this time she was also involved in the movement for women's rights.

Dr. Montessori had a son but the social structure at the time did not allow her to keep him with her as she was unmarried. He was fostered by a family in the countryside and visited by his mother regularly. Dr. Montessori got a job working with children in an asylum for mentally retarded children. With her keen observational powers and her ever curious mind, she became interested in their education as well as their health. She studied the works of Itard and Séguin, who in turn were influenced by Rousseau and Froebel. In order to understand these works fully she spent many long nights translating them from French into Italian! But her study was not in vain. She adapted and devised several educational materials which she used with great success with the children under her care. When they passed examinations, Dr. Montessori asked herself why the children in the regular schools could not reach much higher levels with good educational stimulation.

On 6th January 1907 Dr. Montessori opened her first Casa dei Bambini (Children's House) in Rome. The owners of a large building were concerned about the small children running wild so they invited Dr. Montessori to carry out an experiment with a day nursery for children ranging from 3 to 7 years. She set up a simple room and put in many of the educational materials which she had devised or adapted from others over the previous years. She employed the caretaker's daughter to take care of the children and instructed her not to teach them anything, but rather to allow them to use the materials. She herself observed for long periods and added or took away materials according to how the children were attracted to them. The children were shown how to use the materials and as long as they did not abuse them, were free to use them when they wished.

Within months wonderful things were happening! Children were writing their names, talking about mathematical shapes, behaving very politely and Montessori realized she was making exciting discoveries. People heard about Casa dei Bambini and came to see the children. In a world where children were considered noisy and troublesome, these productive well-behaved little people were seen as a miracle. A second nursery was opened by Dr. Montessori the following year. Within a short time she was well known throughout most countries in Europe. In 1912 she published her first of many books, "The Montessori Method". In 1913 she was invited to the USA where she travelled widely, taking her now fifteen year old son, Mario, with her. There she was welcomed enthusiastically and she set up many

'Montessori' classrooms.

In the meantime she started the training of teachers to carry on her method but at all times she was reluctant to allow this training to pass out of her personal control. She believed that her method was not easy to use correctly because it involved a basic shift in attitude towards children. Her observations were continually leading her to adapt and develop new materials. She started to work on the method for older children (6-12 years) as far back as 1912 but believed that it was too big a task for one person. With the help of various interested people, the 'Advanced Montessori Method' was developed over a period of many years. Dr. Montessori was also interested in the next level (12-18 years) but she did not have time in her busy life to explore it fully, writing only two chapters to explain her ideas. However it has been developed since her death, and in the early years of the twenty first century the Montessori method for adolescents is beginning to grow into a thriving movement.

Montessori worked for some years in Spain and spent all of World War II in India. She finally settled in Holland and there, with the help of her son Mario and his wife, set up a centre for developing the Montessori method. In the latter part of her life, Dr. Montessori's focus went back to the infant and she further developed her ideas on the first years of life. She published "The Absorbent Mind", the book many consider to be her best, in 1949, just a few years before her death, in 1952.

2

An Education for Life

"The child is endowed with unknown powers, which can guide us to a radiant future. If what we really want is a new world, then education must take as its aim the development of these hidden possibilities" *(Montessori, M., The Absorbent Mind, Chapter – The Child's Part in World Reconstruction, 1973)*

Dr. Montessori considered that her 'method' was not an invention but rather a discovery. She had discovered the true nature of the child. It was natural to learn with enthusiasm and to take in knowledge and develop skills with ease. In her society, and to a lesser extent to-day, the belief was that it had to be difficult to learn. Observation of the child had shown Dr. Montessori that, given the right conditions and the freedom to use them, happy learning and the development of a strong healthy personality were the natural heritage of every child.

Dr. Montessori was a strong advocate of world peace but she thought that peace must start from within. She saw that for many adults this required too great a change to happen in one lifetime. She told us we must look to the children and create conditions which would allow them to grow up with inner peace and wisdom. The method focussed on educating children for life rather than for knowledge or employment. The aim of her method is to give children the opportunity to grow into adults, who love life and are at peace with themselves and others. But, she warned us, the only way to do this is to allow the true nature of the child to dictate how he or she grows and learns. And that is the core of what is now called, the Montessori Method.

3
Stages of Development

""Development is a series of rebirths. There comes a time when one psychic personality ends and another begins" " *(Montessori, M., The Absorbent Mind, Chapter – The Periods of Growth 1973)*

One of the basic observations which Dr. Montessori made was that the years of childhood are divided into stages of development - 0-6 years, 6-12 years, 12-18 years and 18-24 years. These ages are reflected in the educational systems in most countries and in many religious customs. Dr. Montessori believed that these stages were radically different from each other and that children go through a kind of metamorphosis as they pass from one to the next. In the same way as a caterpillar changes completely into a butterfly, children change as they pass naturally through growth and development stages of life.

The first period, 0-6 years, is characterised by an absorbent mind, which makes learning apparently effortless. During this time the child goes through much change and his or her development must be protected in a partially closed environment. It is a self-focussed time of life where the main task is to develop the personality. In the protected world that we provide, the child is learning more than in any other period of life. In the first two and a half to three years the child directly absorbs life, language and skills for living. Up to six years they practice what they have learned and gradually make it all conscious. By six years of age the personality has been formed!

The second period, 6-12 years, is characterised by a highly creative imagination and a great interest in the social group. It is a stable time of growing and acquiring knowledge and skills. The child becomes very interested in a much wider environment - most eight year olds would probably fancy a trip to Mars, if Mom or Dad would come along!

The third period, 12-18 years, is again a time of much change. A development of rational thinking is accompanied by huge physical, hormonal and emotional changes. Dr. Montessori suggested that this time is for learning to be an independent adult and for getting plenty of healthy food and fresh air. Children should not be overburdened with academic bookwork in these years - it was much easier to do that between 6 and 12 years, she claimed.

The fourth period, 18-24 years is the time when childhood comes to an end and the young person finds a place in society. Education, formal and informal, continues through this period but now it is not the responsibility of the adult. The child is independent!

4
A Special
Type of Mind

"There is an intense and specialised sensitiveness in consequence of which the things about him awaken so much interest and so much enthusiasm that they become incorporated in his very existence. The child absorbs these impressions not with his mind but with his life itself" <u>*(Montessori, M., The Absorbent Mind, Chapter – The Periods of Growth, 1973)*</u>

The absorbent mind is the centre of much of Dr. Montessori's philosophy about the child in the first six years of life. The child learns by absorbing knowledge effortlessly, like a sponge soaks up water. He is driven to seek experiences in the world around by the *horme* (an inner urge which exists before the will is developed) and those experiences enter his mind through the senses. These are not merely experiences for the child but they create the basic fabric of his personality. Have you ever seen a young child playing with water in the kitchen? She will pour water again and again from the same cup, not noticing the water pouring on the floor. No matter how many times we tell her to leave it alone she will go back for more, until quite suddenly she is satisfied just as though the absorbent mind were full for the time being! All the time that water was being poured information was being stored, not just about water and pouring, but about feelings of satisfaction with work, being in control and concentrating deeply. These are not simply experiences like we as adults get, but they are actually creating the personality of the child.

Apart from the *horme*, mentioned above, the absorbent mind has some other assistants in the task of creating the personality, an important group being what Dr. Montessori called the sensitive periods. These are periods in a child's life when he is particularly drawn to certain stimulii or experiences. These help to create certain functions or skills for the personality. A sensitive period is always temporary and will fade away when no longer required. A good example is the sensitive period for language which lasts up to 6 years of age. A child who learns a language before 6 years will not have difficulty speaking with the correct accent and grammar, whilst those who attempt to learn a second language later know how difficult it can be. The sensitive period has passed. Another example worth noting is the sensitive period for order. Have you ever seen a young child upset because you did not put something in the right place or tell the story in the right sequence? Next time it happens remember that the child is only following the very strong instructions from her sensitive period for order. If she did not hold onto that order she could not manage to make sense of all the information that is coming in during the early years.

There are many sensitive periods and it is important for adults to look out for these so that they may understand what is happening to the child and provide the right things in his environment for that time. There are sensitive periods for language, movement, order, culture and more. When a sensitive period passes the child will develop new interests and move on to develop new skills.

5
Imagination

"We often forget that imagination is a force for the discovery of truth. The mind is not a passive thing, but a devouring flame, never in repose, always in action." *(Montessori, M., The Absorbent Mind, Chapter - Through Culture and the Imagination, 1973)*

The imagination is a powerful tool and children can use this from an early age. We can observe it even in infancy, for example a child knows food coming because he hears the rattle of the fridge door - he is using his imagination. And children of four years of age can imagine places far away when they have seen some pictures and a map. Dr. Montessori stressed that fantasy and imagination were quite different and she did not encourage fantasy especially for children under four or five years, when they cannot distinguish between reality and make believe. However she did encourage stimulating the imagination with interesting information based on reality.

The real power of the imagination comes into force for the child of 6 to 12 years. As the absorbent mind fades away the power of the imagination takes over as the chief means of learning. It allows the child to imagine things far away and long ago, in space and in the future, in a jungle or inside a tiny seed. The fire of imagination drives the child to seek knowledge with a huge thirst. Imagination is the tool which moves the mind from the concrete to the abstract, allowing the child to form ideas about how the world works. It is an important part of the Montessori method both for the 6-12 year olds and for the older adolescents, to present the imagination with exciting facts. Learning should never be boring with such an active imagination. The adult must inspire with the excitement of the cosmos, and that is not difficult! Then the child and the adolescent will learn because they are interested. A teacher does not have to teach, instead the job of the teacher is to open doors to learning and provide structured pathways that the children can follow independently.

6
Montessori Schools & The Prepared Environment

"[The prepared environment's] influence is indirect, but unless it be well done there will be no effective and permanent results of any kind, physical, intellectual or spiritual." (Montessori, M, The Absorbent Mind, Chapter - The Teacher's Preparation, 1973)

Montessori schools are places of learning where the Montessori principles and educational activities are used. They most common age ranges are as follows:

0-1.5 years	Infants
1.5-3 years	Toddlers
3-6 years	Pre-school
6-9 years	Lower school
9-12 years	Middle school
12-15 years	Junior Upper school
15-18 years	Senior Upper school

In these places there will be a "Prepared Environment" - a place which is carefully prepared based on observation of the children's needs. With the guidance of the teacher, the activities and materials available in this prepared environment will help the child to teach herself and to become more independent.

This environment takes much work and preparation by the teacher. He will observe the children every day and change the environment if that is required.   The teacher will keep everything in perfect condition, knowing that it is the key to the child's independence and learning. Within the prepared environment the child works freely with Montessori activities, learning to concentrate and fulfilling her internal needs. The environment is prepared so that it provides natural limits and feedback and the child becomes an independent learner.

However children will not be in class all day in any school - there is break time and outdoor time. But Montessori principles can be applied in any situation for any age group. Whatever the curriculum or whatever the age, freedom, independence and respect plus all the other principles can be applied.

Preschools and schools have programmes and materials built around the Montessori principles. The youngest children (0-3 years) will have detailed routines and activities following the Montessori principles. The adolescent Montessori schools have routines and activities that are relevant to their emerging adult personalities. There are Montessori schools in some parts of the world, where financial circumstances have meant they could afford few Montessori materials. The teachers have had to improvise. But the Montessori principles can be used anywhere by an adult who fully understands the method.

In the following chapters let us find out a little more about these principles.

7
Respect for the Child

"The child can only build well if this help [the parent's] is given in a suitable way. Thus, the authority of parents does not come from a dignity standing on its own feet, but it comes from the help they are able to give their children. The truly great authority and dignity of parents rests solely upon this." (Montessori, M, The Absorbent Mind, Chapter – Education for Life, 1973)

Respect for others and respect for the environment are the rules for children in a Montessori class. Children are free to work in any way that pleases their inner needs but they must follow the basic rules of respect. Likewise the teacher is obliged to respect the child. This respect must be absolute and it requires quite a shift from traditional norms to achieve this.

⇒ The Montessori teacher or parent must respect the child's right to choose, even when it is obviously the wrong choice from an adult point of view. Can you wait while a ten year old rings up to check if there are seats for the concert even though you know it is highly unlikely there will be any left?

⇒ Respect includes allowing the child to make his own mistakes without being corrected. So if your daughter of three is putting her coat on the wrong way can you wait until she finds out herself or do you find yourself driven to jump up and help?

⇒ Respect means being willing to create a place and time where the child's needs come before the adult's. When the children arrive at school in the morning do you greet the child and then start discussing the weather with the parent over his head?

⇒ And one of the most difficult for us as adults to accept is that respect means waiting to be asked before offering praise. How many times are you tempted to say, "Oh! How lovely!" just when she is deeply engrossed in her painting?

(An adult will interfere if the child is in danger of being actually harmed.)

8

Independence & Responsibility

" *If anything is likely to make the character indecisive it is the inability to control matters without having to seek advice.*" (Montessori, M., The Absorbent Mind, Chapter - Mistakes and their correction, 1973)

The child has the right to grow and become independent and it is part of the Montessori philosophy that we stand back and allow this to happen. We will offer guidance and help but wherever possible we will make it possible for the child to do it himself. Thus we preserve his dignity, which is the core of his personality. From letting the nine month old feed herself, through teaching the three year old to blow his own nose, to showing the nine year old how to iron her own blouse, we devise means of making the child independent of us.

Responsibility always goes hand in hand with independence. We as Montessori teachers or parents will always need to give some good example about being responsible 'citizens', picking up litter, clearing our own plates after meals and so on. But responsibility goes even deeper than that. We must allow a child to feel that his life is his own responsibility. If the adult makes all the decisions then the child knows that it is the adult's fault if something goes wrong. The child must make decisions, bigger decisions as she grows older, and must take responsibility for these. If a six year old spends all his money that his uncle gave him in the first shop, we must not replace that money because we feel sorry that he has no money left. Nor should we give lectures about spending, the incident is self-correcting, like many Montessori materials which you will hear about later.

Montessori offered one helpful tool to support independence – the control of error. She showed us how to find a way to let the child find her own mistakes. In that way the child is able to control her own life and early on she learns that her life, her mistakes and her learning are all her own responsibility.

The adult should not confuse "taking blame" with "taking responsibility". If the adult gives her responsibility with respect and guidance, the child finds that it is fun to take control of her own life. Independence and self responsibility are natural.

9
Movement & Activity

"..the child's intelligence can develop to a certain level without the help of his hand. But if it develops with his hand, then the level it reaches is higher, and the child's character is stronger." (Montessori, M., The Absorbent Mind, Chapter - Intelligence and the Hand, 1973).

Freedom of movement is essential for learning, according to Dr. Montessori. In the first three years of life movement is the principal way children learn. Prepared environments for the children under three in Montessori centres are designed around the need for movement - both gross and fine motor movement.

In Montessori classes for all ages, children can work on the floor or at tables, moving arms or legs as they need to. All Montessori materials are designed to involve activity even when learning advanced concepts of grammar and compound multiplication. Montessori wanted the adolescents to spend much time outdoors doing everyday tasks in the fresh air.

Many activities, especially in the pre-school class for 3-6 years, are designed to refine movement. You will see children carefully pouring water from one jug to another, concentrating deeply so that they do not spill a drop! One area of movement which got particular attention from Dr. Montessori was the movement of the hand. She believed that refinement of movement of the hand was central to the development of the brain. She referred to the hand as the instrument of the brain. Montessori activities involve precision of hand movement, from sewing to placing pegs in pegboards to repairing farm machines.

Work with the hand is always deeply connected with concentration, according to Dr. Montessori. When the hand is actively involved the child concentrates and learns more easily. Concentration is the centre of any Montessori programme. The Montessori method provides both activities that attract concentration and the environment where the child will not be interrupted. And so the skill of concentration is built.

10
Freedom & Discipline

"Only through freedom and environmental experience is it practically possible for human development to occur." (Montessori, M., The Absorbent Mind, Chapter – The Child's Conquest of Independence, 1973).

We have mentioned freedom of choice and freedom of movement, yet you will remember that one of the characteristics of the children in the first Children's House was good behaviour and politeness.

If children are bored or frustrated from having their inner needs rejected, they will behave restlessly and their energy will be used for destructive activities. Dr. Montessori found that if children were offered an environment with many opportunities to satisfy their spontaneous needs AND they were offered the freedom to choose to use these opportunities as they needed to, then they were able to direct their energies in a calm constructive manner.

Freedom and discipline are 'two sides of the one medal'. When children are given freedom to choose they have opportunities to practise making choices. This develops their will and so they develop inner self-discipline. Self-discipline is far more effective than discipline imposed by an adult.

We have seen how freedom develops discipline but let us now look at how discipline supports freedom. We have rules in a Montessori class which prohibit interfering with others, damaging the materials and so on. But we try to make it possible for the child to control himself when he breaks rules. The teacher only interferes when the child is out of control or simply does not understand the rule.

The Montessori method works from the basis that a child will not behave badly on purpose if her other needs are being satisfied. However she will make mistakes. Dr Montessori said that we should develop a 'friendly attitude towards error'. We must allow the environment to give feedback. A Montessori environment is carefully structured in an orderly manner so that it is clear where the boundaries are and the child is able to control his own mistakes. The Montessori materials have an inbuilt 'control of error' which is central to their design. It is easy for the child to see what he ought to do and to see his mistakes. His natural reaction is always to do it right next time.

Dr. Montessori disapproved of rewards and punishments. They make the child work for somebody else's motivation. Montessori believed that the joy and satisfaction of work was sufficient for the child to become self-motivated. If we force the child to focus on a reward or a punishment we will divert that motivation. What will happen when we remove the rewards and punishments? There will be no motivation!

Montessori adults are trained to show children how to do things correctly the first time and then to interfere as little as possible. By observing the children carefully they will know when it is necessary to offer help or to occasionally impose discipline. Not only do we manage to have a room of well behaved children by using this system, but more importantly the children preserve their self-esteem and develop an inner discipline. These are character traits which will last them throughout their lives and so we can say we offered a true 'education for life'.

11
Concentration & Social Development

"The first essential for the child's development is concentration. It lays the whole basis for his character and social behaviour. ...... Out of this comes a change, an adaptation, which is nothing if not the birth of social life itself. " <u>(Montessori, M., The Absorbent Mind, Chapter - Social Development, 1973)</u>

Dr. Montessori believed that children are by nature happy and sociable. They are not destructive and noisy unless their basic needs are not being met. Children want to behave well and want to learn if they are allowed to. She referred to the natural state of the child as 'normalised'. She did not mean that there had to be a 'norm' which children must conform to but rather that each child will find his own level of personality which will fit into society if provided with the right conditions.

Children have a very strong drive to do certain things, especially in the first three years. If we block this drive the child becomes frustrated and the energy she had to carry out the activity is used to do something else - maybe something noisy and destructive. Or maybe she becomes very quiet and withdrawn. Dr. Montessori called these deviations. She said most 'bad behaviour' from children was the result of deviations. We the adults have caused these by blocking the child's needs and not removing obstacles from her environment.

However Dr. Montessori said that deviations could be cured, especially before the age of 6 years. If a child is allowed to work, uninterrupted, with things that grab his attention and which he has freely chosen, he will start to concentrate. Then he will become 'normalised' and the deviations disappear. It sounds easy and it is! But it requires a great deal of preparation and change of attitude on the part of the adult. Dr. Montessori suggests that we owe this to the child. It is his right.

This 'normalised' child will be a caring and sociable child. He will want to help others, to share and to have fun. To be a social human being is much easier when one is satisfied within. Children are by nature sociable. They love to be with others. However the first task that nature has given them is to create their own personality and their own skills. They will learn to be sociable when their natural energy is channelled into *purposeful activities* that help them to learn to concentrate and thereby gain control of themselves. If we try to force them to learn to be sociable before they have gained this control, they will resist us, because their nature is telling them to take care of their own personality development first. We, as adults, have to learn to trust that inner sense and give them the freedom to do this.

12
Montessori
Materials & Activities

"..the [teacher] must explain the use of material.   She is, mainly, a connecting link between the material (the objects) and the child." (Montessori, M, The Discovery of the Child, Chapter – The Teacher, 1966)

We mentioned above that the Montessori materials contained an inbuilt control of error and also that they encouraged refinement of hand movement. These materials are designed to support the Montessori principles in action. Montessori materials are designed to develop independence and to provoke activity. They are made simply and beautifully, attracting children to work with them, and they are orderly and precise, developing both logical thinking and creativity.

Not every Montessori activity is a standardised material as ordered from the catalogue. These beautiful items are of great importance but Montessori lessons are on a much wider range of activities. Shaking hands or making a telephone call can be Montessori lessons. We can turn sweeping the floor into a Montessori material by designing the activity so that it supports the Montessori principles. It is always possible to improvise and make our own materials where circumstances demand that. However we must never make the mistake of thinking we do not need materials – at home or in school!

The Montessori materials are the tools by which we allow the child to become independent of adults. We put the focus on the materials and not on the adult. The adult is the link with these activities but the child teaches himself by working with them. Ask a Montessori child who taught her to read and she will usually answer that she taught herself. She has learned to be independent and she understands she is responsible for her own learning. Her self-esteem has been left intact. These are not only important factors in the development of personality but they are also strong motivations to go on learning. We have what is popularly called a "win-win" situation.

The materials are also the way in which children can find purposeful activities upon which to concentrate. Montessori materials and exercises are designed to allow concentration. Without opportunities to concentrate, children are unable to develop character, will, self-control. They will never find the road to independence!

These materials take much careful preparation on the part of the adult. The adult gives attention to making these suitable for the child's needs according to Montessori principles and then his/her job in 'teaching' the children is made much easier. In fact that is the Montessori teacher's job – preparing activities and showing the child how to use them. In a traditional system the teacher teaches and uses objects or materials to help her to teach. A Montessori teacher prepares objects or materials and shows the child how to teach himself through these objects.

13
The Montessori Adult

"*The [adult's] skill in not interfering comes with practice…. It means rising to spiritual heights. True spirituality realises that even to help can be a source of pride. The real help that the [adult] can give does not lie in obeying a sentimental impulse, but it comes from subjecting one's love to discipline, using it with discernment…*" <u>*(Montessori, M., The Absorbent Mind, Chapter - The Teacher's Preparation, 1973)*</u>

By now you have discovered that it is challenging but exciting work to be a Montessori teacher or a Montessori parent. Adults must learn to stand back and not interfere, yet they must observe what is going on. Environments and materials must be prepared and kept updated and in good condition. If you are a parent or a teacher you will know that observation is actually quite difficult to do yet it is central to being a useful adult in the child's life. Let us look briefly at the work a Montessori adult must do, outer and inner.

The adult, as we said, gives much attention to preparing and maintaining the environment. This includes the room, the materials and the adult himself. A Montessori teacher must learn and know the exercises very well because he must give lessons all the time. He is the dynamic link between the child and the environment. He spends time observing the children and taking action according to this. It may involve changing the environment, giving lessons to certain children or dealing with a conflict between children which *they have not been able to solve* themselves. The correct action becomes apparent when the adult observes.

Parents will not keep the environment totally focussed on the children because they are dealing with a family home where different age groups have needs. However they can prepare activities for the children and should maintain an attractive and orderly environment so that the children are able to use these activities. Most importantly, parents should observe all the time and they will soon discover many of their children's real needs.

The adult has an even bigger task than preparing the environment. She must prepare herself, spiritual preparation, as Dr. Montessori called it. She must examine her basic attitudes to children and many other things in life and change these. Deep respect for the children involves not interfering, sitting still and observing for long periods, moving quietly and unobtrusively about the room when the child is concentrating, not dominating, being willing to hand over control and admitting one's own mistakes. Parents will be more relaxed at home but the same principles of observing, not interfering, not dominating and admitting mistakes apply whether you are a teacher or a parent!

Be careful, whether you are a parent or a teacher, not to abandon the children when you first learn to stand back. Children do need guidance and should never be allowed to behave in a way that interferes with the rights of others.

All of this involves quite radical changes in attitude for most of us. We may know in our minds that these principles make sense but we have been conditioned by our society and our reactions to situations may not be what we planned. Inner spiritual preparation is just as important as learning about the Montessori materials when you are training to be a Montessori teacher. If you are a parent, your own inner preparation is probably the most important gift you can give your child.

Dr. Montessori believed that becoming a Montessori teacher was actually more difficult for those that were already trained as traditional teachers than it was for those trained in, for instance, science or engineering! Can you imagine why she thought that?

She believed that parents in our society tend to take over and impose their own personalities on their children. She realised most of us do that out of love but she said we must become aware of the damage we do to the child's natural spontaneous joy in life and learning when we behave in that way.

It is not easy to make these changes but when you examine it honestly you will see how important it is for adults to change themselves and their attitudes before they try to influence children. It is hard work but you will never be bored. And you will feel a great satisfaction and joy when you see how your work helps the children to grow up happy and confident!

14
Montessori & the Way Forward

"It is not right to say the mother and father have made their child. Rather we should say: 'The child is the father of the man.' " *(Montessori, M., The Secret of Childhood, Chapter - Order, 1966)*

Dr. Montessori died in 1952 but her philosophy is ever more relevant at the dawn of the new millennium. The world is changing rapidly, people's lives are changing rapidly and what is needed from education is a format for helping people to cope with all this change. Research is moving forward so fast that it is impossible for any individual to keep up to date except in a specialised area. What children need to take from their education is the skill to learn all the time, an interest in learning and the self-confidence and self-discipline to manage this learning. The Montessori method has offered one of the means of filling this need and that explains the upsurge in popularity for Montessori education in the last few decades.

On the 6th January 2007 it was 100 years since the opening of the first Casa dei Bambini in Rome. There are many thousands of Montessori schools throughout the world in every continent. Montessori principles are gradually being absorbed into the education systems of the world but as a society we have a long way to go to fully understand the depth of respect for children that Dr. Montessori demanded.

When children are allowed to grow up at peace within, they will become fulfilled, happy and peaceful adults who love to learn and love to help others. Dr. Montessori claimed that is the only to change the world. It is too late to change the adults. We must start with the children!